*Love you*
*Judy*
*Ps. 127:1*

# Trust in Times of Trouble

## Spiritual Poems and Scriptures
### by Judith Asmus Hill

PublishAmerica
Baltimore

First printing

All scripture quotes taken from the King James Version.

ISBN: 1-60672-612-9
PUBLISHED BY PUBLISHAMERICA, LLLP
www.publishamerica.com
Baltimore

Printed in the United States of America

# DEDICATION

This book of poems and scriptures is dedicated to all those who need to know that they can trust the Lord in every situation because He is always faithful.

Much love to you.

Judy

# ACKNOWLEDGMENTS

I would like to thank my Savior and Lord for seeing me through the year and a half of my husband Dean's illness and the 2 years of loneliness after he went to heaven. These poems were birthed out of that difficult time which gave the hope to carry on.

I would also like to thank my family and friends who were there with helping hands as well as many prayers! I also appreciate the care and encouragement that my new husband, Jim, is giving me as I finalize this poem book: *Trust in Times of Trouble*.

My love to each of you.

Judy

# CONTENTS

# TRUST IN TIMES OF TROUBLE

Deep calls out to deep
When troubles come
Your way
So call out Father's name
In nighttime or noonday.

His power will
Sustain you—
Never fear or doubt.
Angels will take
Care of you
They are round about.

God will hear
And send you aid
Fix eyes on Him—
Don't be afraid.

When the storm
Has passed…
Blue skies again
You'll see.
Don't forget
To thank Him—
It will set you free.

*The Lord is my light and my salvation, whom shall I fear? The Lord is the strength of my life; of whom shall I be afraid?*
Psalm 27:1

# SEEK GOD'S PLAN

I have an open door
For you...
If you will seek to find.
I have a special
Path for you
It's always on my Mind.

Your journey takes
A lifetime.
Each process
Is a plan.
The highway has
It's curves.
But you will say.
"God can,"

Your steps are
Like no other—
Don't compare
With any brother.

There's a map that's
Always right—
Seek My Word
You'll have your sight.

*Call unto me and I will answer thee and show thee great and mighty things
which thou knowest not.*
Jeremiah 33:3

# THE LIGHT OF HIS LOVE

There's a crown of light
Upon your head
It's sent from heaven above.
Those who walk in darkness
Will feel that crown as love.

When hard times come
They'll look to you.
They'll want you by their side
It's at that time of need, you see.
You'll help them to abide.

If you abide in Me—
I will abide in you.
That's a promise from His word.
It is tried and true.

*Blessed is the people that know the joyful sound: they shall walk, O Lord,
in the light of Thy countenance.*
Psalm 89:15

# WHAT MATTERS FOR ETERNITY

The time of life is fleeting
Be careful what you do.
What matters for eternity
Is what I've planned for you.

I am your God, I am your life
Let go of worry, doubt or strife.
Spend time with Me—
And you will see
How great your life will be.

Don't carry others' burdens
Give them all to Me.
I can handle any need
If My voice you'll heed.

*But seek ye first the kingdom of God, and His righteousness; and all these things shall be added unto you.*
Matthew 6:33

# TAKE GOD'S WAY

When you are tired
And need a rest—
Sit down a while
And give your best.

Give your best
In prayer to Me.
Life looks better
You will see.

Don't carry your burdens
Another day—
My yoke is easy
At My side you'll stay.

My ways are higher
Just wait and know.
At the end of yourself
My way you'll go.

*For My yoke is easy, and my burden is light.*
Matthew 11:30

# MY GREATEST FRIEND

Jesus is my
Greatest friend
He's there through
Thick and thin—
He'll be there to
Comfort you
If you will let Him in.

"Jesus, come into
My heart,"
Is a prayer that
I have said—
He's there with me
In darkest night.
When I lay
Down in bed.

He sticks closer
Than a brother
His ways are like
No other—
He died upon a cross
To save me from my sin.
The stripes upon His back
Bring healing from within.

He's my friend
In every trial—
Just His name
Will make me smile.

*And the peace of God which passes all understanding, shall keep your hearts and minds through Christ Jesus.*
Philippians 4:7

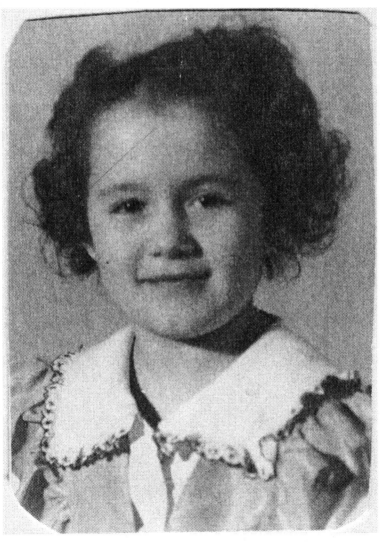

Judy Frobose (Asmus Hill)—age about 6
Raised as a country farm girl near Pemberville, Ohio.
With 4 sisters and 2 brothers

# HEARING GOD'S VOICE

At the end of a day
No one is here.
I turn on the TV
To have some cheer.
Christian music
Lifts my soul.
It gets in my heart
And makes me whole.

Then I take my pen
And hear God's voice.
There's much to do
I've made my choice.
The choice I've made
To sit at His feet.
Is the best one to make
The Master to meet.

He tells me and warns me
Of things to come.
Then I'll be ready, prepared
And then some….
So whether alone
Or in a crowd.
His still small voice
Is very loud.

*Be still and know that I am God.*
Psalm 46

# "HURRY UP, LORD"

Many times
I'd like to say
"Hurry up, Lord,"
When I pray.
But then I know
That time is dear.
When trials come
God is near.

It's in the valleys
That we grow.
How much....
We'll never know.
The shaping and
Molding by His hand.
His Spirit is there
To help us stand.

There's something cleansing
About my tears.
They can wash away
Many fears—
At the strangest times
My tears will flow.
Can't hold them back
Let others know—

Let them know
What's in your heart.
In hard times
They'll do their part.

*Rejoicing in hope; patient in tribulation; continuing instant in prayer.*
Romans 12:12

# NO OTHER WAY

There is so much
Busyness in life.
It's easy to
Give in to strife.

Then I stop to ponder
At end of day—
Don't let this time
Just pass away.

I want to make
The most of time.
Not just mundane
No reason or rhyme.

I want to lift
My vision high.
Take my Lord's hand
And stay nearby.

Stay near His side
No other way.
"Lord please help me
Trust and obey."

*In all thy ways, acknowledge Him, and He shall direct they paths.*
Proverbs 3:6

# MY GOOD SHEPHERD

Waiting is so hard to do
It tests my patience
Through and through.
It's quite a process
Day by day.
Only the Lord
Can help me pray.

At times I only
want to ask…
But I must listen
That is my task.
He speaks to me
In time of need.
He gives a word
That I will heed—

When I'm in doubt
And want to pout.
He's always there
To help me out.
He's my good shepherd
He sets me free.
He leads me on
And helps me see.

*I am the good shepherd, and know My sheep, and am known of mine.*
John 10:14

# HEAVEN'S TOUCH

It helps to know that others
Are praying for you.
Then you'll surely feel that
You will make it through.

There're days when doubts
Are heavy…
Making sad your heart.
The Lord then leads someone
To pray their part.

Then the load is lifted
To a higher plain.
Your faith soon returns
Tears are dried again.

You'll never know til glory
Until He tells your story.
How your prayers
Availed much.
You took the time
With heaven's touch.

*The effectual fervent prayer of a righteous man availeth much.*
James 5:16

# JUST KEEP SMILING

When you want
To wear a frown
And your world
Seems upside down….

JUST KEEP SMILING

When the bills
Keep piling in
Don't forget to
Wear a grin.

JUST KEEP SMILING

When the doctor says.
"It doesn't look good,"
On God's report
You've always stood.

JUST KEEP SMILING

A merry heart's a medicine
So let the laughter roll.
Find a friend who's funny
And let joy takes its toll.

JUST KEEP SMILING

*A merry heart doeth good like a medicine: but a broken spirit drieth the bones.*
Proverbs 17:22

# THY WORD IS SO SWEET

If you're looking for comfort
In time of need…
Just open the Bible
Begin to read.

The Word will revive you
Make you brand new…
Healing your need
God's help will come through.

His Word changes never
There's help there forever.
The more you read…
The better you'll feel.
So eat good portions
At every meal—

God's Word is so sweet
Like honey to taste…
I'll read His Word
There's no time to waste.

*How sweet are Thy words unto my taste! Yea, sweeter than honey to my mouth.*
Psalm 119:103

Judy Frobose marries Dean Asmus on July 22, 1961

# MY HUSBAND, MY LOVE

My husband is
My dearest friend
He's always there for me.
Even when he's feeling ill
He's there to help me see—

He wants to help me see that
Trials come to make us strong.
After all is said and done
We'll join the heavenly throng.

Our song will be to God above
His praises we will sing with love
My life has ever been so sweet—
My husband's made my life complete.

We asked the Lord into our heart
Made a covenant not to part
In sickness or in health…
Poverty or wealth
Our love will be forever!

*And walk in love, as Christ also has loved us and given Himself for us,*
*an offering and a sacrifice to God for a sweet smelling aroma.*
Ephesians 5:2

# OVERWHELMING DAYS

Some days seem
overwhelming—
You think
You're going to quit.

Life's race has
Crushing blows
Right when the
Storm has hit.

But then the Lord
Sends someone—
To lift those
Hands for you.

They come right in
And give you help.
There's much that
They will do.

It's not just what
They do.
It's how they make
You feel—
It's the love of Jesus
In their heart
You know that
It is real.

*Beloved let us love one another, for love is of God;*
I John 4:7

# YOUR ONLY FOUNDATION

When hurricanes come
And strong winds blow…
Have your roots grown deep
From the Word that you know.

Will your life be uprooted
Your heart filled with fear
Will you press into Jesus
And know that He's near.

When all earthly things
Have been blown away
What will be left
In your life to stay.

Nothing else matters
When life brings frustration
Trust in the Lord…
Your only foundation!

*For no other foundation can anyone lay than that which is laid, which is Jesus Christ.*
1 Corinthians 3:11

# IF WE DIDN'T HAVE THE RAIN

It never is convenient
On a day of rain
We long for the sunshine
To light our face again.

The flowers we would never smell
Our own sweet story ever tell...

IF WE DIDN'T HAVE THE RAIN

When trials come and troubles face
It's hard to see the end of race
We never know what good we've done
Lead some to Christ, they watch us run...

IF WE DIDN'T HAVE THE RAIN

When others see you keep on trusting
Even when the storm keeps busting
They watch you as you keep on praying
Soon they'll ask, "What keeps you staying?

IF WE DIDN'T HAVE THE RAIN

You'll tell them then of Jesus' love
It's working here, not just above.

*Fight the good fight of faith, lay hold on eternal life, whereunto thou art also called, and hast professed a good profession before many witnesses.*
I Timothy 6:12

"Calming the Storms"—cover photo for their 4th Asmus Family Singers CD

# THE FORK IN THE ROAD

In the valley of decision
Uncertainty is there
It brings you into turmoil
You bow your knees in prayer.

You ask the Lord.
"What should I do?"
You wait and listen
He speaks to you.

God speaks to your spirit
If you listen you will hear it
He uses circumstances—
To move you here and there
A word from the Word
Shows you of His care.

He doesn't want to leave you
At the fork in the road
He will use whatever's
Needed with the help
Of his goad.

So seek and you will find
Knock, it shall be opened
And know that your best
Is on His mind.

*Ask, and it shall be given you; seek, and ye shall find; knock, and it shall
be opened unto you.*
Matthew 7:7

# A BEND IN OUR PATHWAY

When you walk
Down a pathway—
It's nice to see the end.
But many times
You cannot see—
Because there is a bend

A bend in our pathway may
Not be what we've planned
But in His mighty purpose.
He guides us by His hand.

Sometimes our hearts
Are filled with fright
When we can't fully
See the light.

The Word's a lamp
Unto our feet—
A light unto our path
When Satan sees us
In God's word.
It sends him into wrath—

So never fear
A bend in the road
God will be there
To lighten the load.

*Thy word is a lamp unto my feet and a light unto my path.*
Psalm 119:105

# THANK GOD FOR NEIGHBORS

Sometimes you feel
Like you're out on a limb
No where to turn—
Tears to the brim

There's a knock at the door
You open it wide—
Your neighbors are there
You ask them inside.

There's food in their hands
A smile on their face.
You know at that time
The Lord sent His grace.

The next day you wonder
How the lawn will be kept
Before you could worry
Your neighbor had swept

He swept through with mower
Quickly and neat.
My heart began dancing
And so did my feet

God shows His love
Through wonderful neighbors
They give of their time—
With the love of their labors.

When we're down from the limb
And our lives rearranged
we want to be neighbors—
Their lives to change.

*Thou shalt love thy neighbor as thyself.*
Romans 13:9

# THE DRAGONFLY

My wonderful husband
was very sick
My heart cried out.
God said "I'll pick.
I will pick his time of healing
Do not let your mind be reeling."

Many times before my face
A Dragon Fly would come.
Getting my attention…
As its wings would hum.

The Dragonfly would hover
Just as if to be a cover.
I knew the Lord above
Was using that as love.

When I found out the nickname
Of this very special creature.
It surely gave a lesson
From this humble science teacher.

The Dragonfly's
A darning needle
Stitching here and there.
Healing will be coming…
Now I know he's in God's care.

When I am least expecting
A dragonfly will hover....
Then I know God's stitching
From one end to the other!

*For I will restore health unto thee, and I will heal thee of they wounds,*
*saith the Lord.*
Jeremiah 30:17

# A GIVING HEART

*Do you want to have a giving heart*
One where you will do your part?

Take the time to love and pray
A special place throughout your day.

Take the time with heaven's touch
You'll find your heart will give out much

Soon your life is a thing of the past.
Only what's done for Christ will last.

Where your treasure is your heart will be
Set treasures in heaven and be set free.

*But lay up for yourselves treasures in heaven, where neither moth nor*
*rust doth corrupt, and where thieves do not break through nor steal: For*
*where your treasure is, there will your heart be also.*
Matthew 6:20, 21

# GOD'S FLOWERS

I'm so glad God gave us flowers
To make our sad hearts warm
We can see His hand extended
He comforts in our storm.

When I've had times of illness
Flowers brought much cheer
It made me see creation
God's love was very near.

God uses many people
To extend to us His love.
The creation of His flowers
Were made in heaven above.

Every time you give God's flowers
Others' hearts are blessed
Always know He sent the showers
God will always give His best.

God always loves through people
So be a vessel fair.
Forget not to send flowers
With God's fragrance in the air.

*Be kindly affectioned one to another with brotherly love; in honor
preferring one another.*
Romans 12:10

# THE RIVER OF GOD

The river of God is fair to be seen
It flows on forever, in this we glean
It never runs dry, day in or day out
Flows through God's children to keep them from doubt.

If we take time to bathe in God's wonderful word
It washes us clean, no discouragement heard.
God pours us the drink that freely gives
The joy of salvation; forever it lives.

The woman at the well accepted this drink
In dire need, she could only think…
She knew she'd been thirsty and very dry
She opened her heart and began to cry.

Many are out there; they need to step in
Into the river, be set free from sin.
Only the river of God will suffice
His only Son, Jesus has paid the price.

*But whosoever drinketh of the water that I shall give him shall never
thirst; but the water that I shall give him shall be in him a well of water
springing up into everlasting life.*
John 4:14

*Not by works of righteousness which we have done, but according to His
mercy He saved us, by*
*the washing of regeneration, and renewing of the Holy Ghost.*
Titus 3:5

# MY MOUNTAIN PRAYER

Lord, in my mountain, I see your hand
Strong and steady helping me stand.
There're days my mountain seems unbearable
Some days, it doesn't seem so terrible.

It's so amazing how my attitude can change
When I take time, Lord, to let You rearrange
To rearrange my thinking that's not always good
When I take time to listen and know You've understood.

Your Word said there'd be many afflictions
But we would recover because of convictions
Convictions in knowing that You would be there
Deliverance is coming, we will not despair!

*Many are the afflictions of the righteous but the lord delivereth him out of them all.*
Psalm 34:19

Last family portrait of the Dean & Judy Asmus family on Christmas Day,
prior to Dean's home going, 2/3/2006

# THE BLESSINGS OF FAMILY

My family is so precious
One of a kind.
No greater joy on earth
What a find.

When one is down
The others care.
They come and help
It is so rare.

In this busy life
They give their time.
They give without
Reason or rhyme.

I thank my God
Day after day.
That He's blessed me
In such a way.

The blessings of family
For this I sing.
I know if I needed
They'd give everything.

*That I may publish with the voice of thanksgiving, and tell of all thy*
*wondrous works.*
Psalm 26:7

# THE LORD SAYS IT'S TIME

It's time for you to come to Me
Your life on earth is finished, you see.
That's what the Father said to my man
Fulfilled your purpose, carried out My plan.

I know that those who grieve for you
Will miss you sorely through and through.
But I have a plan for their lives, too.
They must focus on Me to know what to do.

It's surely My presence that they must seek
Without this, much havoc they will reek.
Lives here on earth are just on loan
They can't depend on the strength of their own.

*For this God is our God for ever and ever: He will be our guide even unto death.*
Psalm 48:14

# A PRAYER DURING SORROW

Dear Lord, my heart is aching sore
It has been pricked right to the core.
The one that I loved is no longer here
So many good memories when he was near.

The day we first met, it was truly your plan
I couldn't have asked for a better man
Not perfect, forgiven through Your cross
Great father and husband, worked hard for his boss.

Every day he laid down his life
Read the Bible to contend with the strife.
The year of his illness, we trusted in You
We believed for a healing through and through.

A number of days before home he went
Lord, your sign truly was heaven-sent.
The dove or the angel's bright feathers that flew
Right through our bedroom, surely were true.

The sign that his life here on earth was finished
It's helped me tremendously, sorrow diminished.
So even at times my heart is still sad
Knowing it's Your plan, makes my heart glad.

*This is my comfort in my affliction: for thy Word hath quickened me.*
Psalm 119:50

# SET YOUR HEART ON HEAVEN

My heart is set on Heaven ever since that day
The day my best friend, husband went along that way.

The angels came to get him, soaring quickly there
He's safely in the arms of Jesus, never to despair.

There's only joy and peace in that glorious heavenly place
It must be so amazing to see Jesus face to face.

I want to tell more people of Jesus' saving grace.
When your heart is open, He'll fill that special space.

So set your heart on heaven, the best is coming soon
When your work is done, He'll take you morning, night ,or noon.

*Set your affection on things above, not on things on the earth. For ye are*
*dead, and your life is hid with Christ in God.*
Colossians 3:2, 3

# IN THE MIDST OF TURMOIL

In the midst of turmoil we may not see clearly
We feel overwhelmed, like quitting so nearly.

We've cried out to God and asked His advice
And then we're surprised when He seems so nice.

Sometimes we expect God to be like our father
Who's at times so busy, we feel like a bother.

The Lord's always reaching just to help us
Why do we waste time to worry and fuss?

He's a Lord who cares more than we know
He'll send those to help us as we go.

*Casting all your care upon Him; for He careth for you.*
I Peter 5:7

# PRAYER FOR PROTECTION

Now that I'm a widow, Lord
I'll need protection only you can afford.
When my husband was alive
I trusted him, I didn't strive.

But now I'm trusting more in You
You'll send angels, their work to do.
Every night when I'm alone
I'll fall asleep; You're on Your throne.

I do not fear, for You are near
Your Word shows that very clear.
Psalm 91 is a comfort to me
I claim each verse and look to Thee.

*Therefore shall no evil befall thee neither shall any plague come nigh thy*
*dwelling. For He shall give His angels charge over thee, to keep thee in*
*all thy ways.*
Psalm 91:10, 11

# IT STILL HURTS

A year and a half
Has slowly slipped by.
A widow I am and I still cry.

When the love of your life
Is no longer here…
It is only the Lord
That sees each tear.

Grieving is different
For each, we know.
Some let go early
And for others it's slow.

But however you deal
With the loss of a spouse…
It can get lonely
They're not in your house.

Then I'm reminded
That Jesus is near.
I go to His Word
He gives me cheer.

I'm waiting to see if
The Lord brings a friend…
A wonderful man
That I could love 'til the end.

God only wants
What is best for me…
My heart's desire
His will to be.

*And call upon Me in the day of trouble: I will deliver thee, and thou shalt glorify Me.*
Psalm 50:15

# BELIEVE

Many times life takes a turn
It wasn't what you thought.
It's time to turn the light on
In the darkness where you sought.

You sought to have belief
In the deepness of your heart.
You wanted God to take charge
Of each and every part.

Even though it's different
Than the way you prayed I'd be.
Trust in God's great plan
Not the picture that you see.

*Trust in the Lord with all thine heart; and lean not unto thine own understanding.*
Proverbs 3:5

"Singing the Word" music CD cover photo, that Judy recorded in their
log home while Dean was ill. She would play this when Dean was
having trouble breathing, and it would calm his anxiety.

# A SONG OF THANKS

Let a song greet you
Morning, night or noon.
It will lift your heart along
Help will come real soon.

A song of thanks in trials
Will help to move a mountain.
It will bubble up inside of you
Just like a flowing fountain.

When in the night
Sleep escapes...
A song will light your room.
It will help you fall asleep
And will destroy the gloom.

*Sing unto the Lord a new song; for He hath done marvelous things.*
Psalm 98:1

# DON'T FEAR

When you wake up in the night
And your heart is filled with fear.

Talk to Father God
'Cause He is always near.

Let the Word of truth transform you
It will comfort through and through.

The Lord speaks through His Word
"Do not fear," is what you've heard.

Let the Word of faith be near you
Speak it with a shout.

Fear and doubt will leave you It throws it all right out.

*Fear thou not; for I am with thee: be not dismayed; for I am thy God: I
will strengthen thee; yea I will help thee; yea I will uphold thee with the
right hand of my righteousness.*
Isaiah 41:10

# THANK GOD IT'S MORNING

It's been a night of tossing and turning
One where your heart has been moving and churning.

The enemy has had his fun
He's talked to you, had you on the run.

You gave in to worry and also to fear
You forgot to remember that the Lord was near.

"Thank God it's morning," your words came with glee
Then you claim victory as quick as can be.

Victory's in Jesus, why didn't I see?
In the darkness of night, I can still be free.

*Peace I leave with you, my peace I give unto you: not as the world giveth,*
*give I unto you. Let not your heart be troubled, neither let it be afraid.*
John 14:27

# TIRED AND WORN

It's the end of your day
What can you say?

So tired and worn…
Your soul has been torn.

Some sadness of loss
Your heart feels a toss.

Memories burned…
Plans yet unturned.

Only Jesus is there
Your mind to repair.

When you can't see his hand…
On His Word you must stand.

*Seek the Lord and His strength seek His Face continually.*
I Chronicles 16:11

# FIGHT THE GOOD FIGHT

There are so many battles
That face us each day...
At times we can only
Cry out and pray.

The Lord requires
Only our best.
If we obey, He'll do
All the rest.

So fight the good fight
Of faith to the end.
Jesus, our captain.
His help He will send.

*You shall not fear them: for the Lord your God, He shall fight for you.*
Deuteronomy 3:22

# DON'T GIVE UP

In the middle of the storm
You'd like to give up.
You've cried out to God,
"Please fill my cup!"

You feel like you're empty
There's nothing inside.
You tried to smile
But instead you cried.

Unto the hills.
You lifted your eyes…
For surely the Lord
Has heard your cries.

Then someone called
Said, "I want to be there."
God answered prayer
And sent those that care.

*I will lift up mine eyes unto the hills, from whence cometh my help. My help cometh from the Lord, which made heaven and earth.*
Psalm 121:1, 2

# DIG DEEP WELLS

Don't wait to dig your well
'Til you're thirsty and dry.
It will then be too late
So why even try?

You must dig deep wells
To prepare for the draught.
If you wait 'til you need it
You'll surely get caught.

Each day of your life
There's choices you make.
If you choose to dig wells
Some good time it will take.

Then when the days
Get really rough…
You've dug in God's Word
And it's more than enough.

Take time with Jesus
Every day.
It's like digging a well
That won't leak away.

*Therefore with joy shall ye draw water out of the wells of salvation. And
in that day shall ye say, Praise the Lord, call upon His name, declare His
doings among the people, make mention that His name is exalted.*
Isaiah 12:3, 4

# I DON'T UNDERSTAND

Things happen in life that
I don't understand
It's at those times
I take hold of God's hand.

His Word is so comforting
And always ready
It's waiting there…
So strong and steady.

If we never had times
Where we had to trust
We wouldn't know…
That spending time is a must.

So I spend time with Jesus
When I don't understand
He's always there…
With His loving hand.

*Thy Words were found, and I did eat them; And Thy Word was unto me
the joy and rejoicing
Of mine heart: for I am called by Thy name, Oh Lord God of hosts.*
Jeremiah 15:16

# DON'T GET DISCOURAGED

When dreams are broken
And life looks grim…
You've gone down for the third time
Trying to swim.

Don't be discouraged
Help is on the way.
Expect provision
At the end of the day.

The Lord has been working
Even though you don't see.
Trust in His promises
Surely to be.

*Trust in Him at all times; ye people, pour out your heart before Him: God is a refuge for us.*
Psalm 62:8

*When I cry unto Thee, then shall mine enemies turn back: this I know; for God is for me.*
Psalm 56:9

# THE TAPESTRY OF LIFE

Our Lord is a weaver
Just look and see.
His plan is so awesome
For you and for me.

He knows exactly
What's best for you.
Just let Him take over
He'll know what to do.

God weaves in and out
Each strand of your life.
He knows how to bring
You the best husband or wife.

The tapestry of life
Is different for all.
A beautiful picture
If on His name you call.

*For I know the thoughts that I think toward you, saith the Lord, thoughts of peace, and not of evil, to give you an expected end. Then shall ye call upon me, and ye shall go and pray unto me, and I will hearken unto you. And ye shall seek me, and find me, when ye shall seek for Me with all your heart.*
Jeremiah 29:11-13

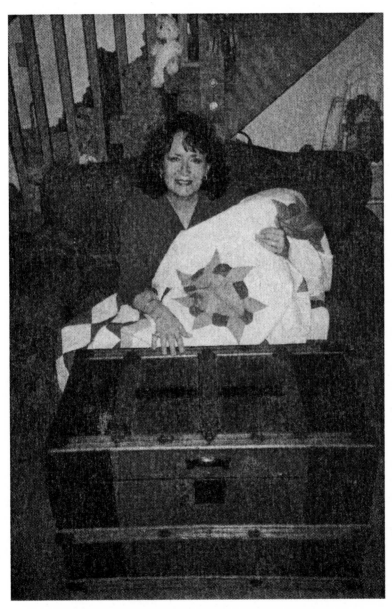

"The Patchwork of Life" music CD cover photo
which included a miraculous family quilt story.

# PRAYER ON A CLOUDY DAY

Lord, here I am again, waiting for the sun
It's hard to start my day, it's just no fun.

But there's really something, truly
When my life is so unruly.
Something's special 'bout a gloomy day
It makes me want to take the time to pray.

I know that there is sunshine in your word
When I take the time to listen, joy is heard.
You, Lord, are the Word alive
In your presence then, I do not strive.

So, Lord, I am okay when skies are gray
For you are all my joy, my sunshine's ray!

*Thou wilt show me the path of life: in Your presence is fullness of joy; at thy right hand there are pleasures for evermore.*
Psalm 16:11

# SERVE WITH GLADNESS

When the Lord speaks to you
And prompts you to serve.
Don't try to dodge it
Go around it or swerve.

Each one is called
To be a servant in life
To humble oneself
It helps with all strife.

You have to know when
It's God that will speak....
If you try to please man
Much havoc you'll wreak.

He never requires
More than you're able
If you depend on yourself
You'll be unstable.

So serve with gladness
When you find out His will.
You can't do it all
Find out; just be still.

*And whatsoever ye do, do it heartily, as to the Lord, and not unto men;
Knowing that of the Lord ye shall receive the reward of the inheritance;
for ye serve the Lord Christ.*
Colossians 3:23, 24

# GOD'S RAINBOW

A rainbow is a sign of peace
From a God who really cares.
When the rain comes, the sunshine, too
It will bring many stares.
People stare into the sky
Just to see this sight.
It strikes a special feeling
When they see the colors bright.
The rainbow is a promise
Given from above.
It will never change
It's a sign of God's great love.
When I see a rainbow
I listen with my heart…
To see if God is giving me
A promise, that's His part.
God made a promise years ago
And He has kept it true.
There's many other promises
That He will keep for you.
The times I've seen God's rainbow
My faith gets a release…
Something I've been praying for
I then can find His peace.

*The rainbow shall be seen in the cloud: And I will remember my covenant, which is between me and you and every living creature of all flesh; and the waters shall no more become a flood to destroy all flesh.*
Genesis 9:14b, 15

*Thou wilt keep him in perfect peace whose mind is stayed on Thee, because he trusteth in Thee.*
Isaiah 26:3

# PRAYER FOR JOY

Lord, I'm so thankful
That my joy, you are
If I depend on others
My joy won't go far.

Some days I'm weary
No strength at all...
It's at those times
On your name I call.

Fear and worry
Come far too often
The blows from the enemy
You will soften.

Your joy is my strength
Each day of my life.
In Your hand are pleasures
To help in my strife.

*For this day is holy unto our Lord; neither be ye sorry; for the joy of the
Lord Is your strength.*
Nehemiah 8:10

# LEARN FROM ME, SAYS THE LORD

The ways of the world
Are not My plan.
It's easy to embrace
The plans of man.

If you talk to Me.
Then wait for revelation
I will put things in your
Heart for explanation.

Go to My Word.
It's always your guide
It's like having Me
Right by your side.

You'll never go wrong
If you obey My word
It's truly the best learning
You've ever heard.

*Teach me, oh Lord, the way of Thy statutes; and I shall keep it unto the end. Give me understanding and I shall keep Thy law; yea, I shall observe it with my whole heart.*
Psalm 119:33, 34

# REMEMBERING PRAYER

It's almost dusk; the sun will set real soon
It's been a lonely day, welcome is the moon.
It means that nighttime rest will still my heart
Remembering my love has gone, forever to depart.

I feel much joy; my loved one is with You
Your word will be my comfort through and through.
Remembering the days gone by...
Dear Lord, You'll help and I will try.

I will try, in You to put my trust
Your constant presence is a must.
I focus on Your love for me
Remembering the cross sets me free.

*I will not leave you comfortless; I will come to you.*
John 14:18

*He healeth the broken heart, and bindeth up their wounds.*
Psalm 147:3

Judy with her husband, Dean, a photo of the last day
that he sat in his special chair on Jan. 29, 2006.

# THE EMPTY CHAIR

In the corner sits a chair
It once was filled with loving care.

The one whose presence sat upon…
Cared for others from dusk to dawn.

That empty chair speaks volumes there
The things he stood for are so rare.

He stood for truth and honesty.
Those things did not come naturally.

The only way he could succeed
Turned to Jesus, His voice to heed.

From his empty chair, if he could speak…
He would tell us all, "Continue to seek.

Seek to follow our Father above.
Your life will be filled with precious love."

*The Lord also will be a refuge for the oppressed A refuge in times of trouble. And they that know thy name will put their trust in Thee: for thou, Lord, hast not forsaken them that seek thee.*
Psalm 9:9-10

*And to know the love of Christ, which passeth knowledge, that ye might be filled with all the*
*fullness of God.*
Ephesians 3:19

# PRAYER DURING LONELINESS

Some days my heart is sad
And I feel so alone.
Then I try to lift my spirits.
Try to do it on my own.

I soon begin to realize
That I'm having no success.
Eating food or watching TV
Doesn't bring me happiness.

It may help for a while
But sadness soon emerges.
It comes in like a wildfire
Like a wind that surges.

Then I begin to praise Him
My heart begins to melt.
My joy is soon returning
God's presence then is felt.

Soon I read the Bible
David had a saddened face.
His spirits, too, were lifted
He sang songs about God's grace.

*O sing unto the Lord a new song; for he hath done marvelous things: His right hand, and His holy arm, hath gotten us the victory.*
Psalm 98:1

*Be of good courage, and He shall strengthen thine heart, all ye that hope in the Lord.*
Psalm 31:24

# A PRAYER IN HARD TIMES

My heart is so heavy
My Lord, be my levy.
Hold back the tide
Of the enemy's ride.

I feel so alone
My mind seems like stone.
I'd like to be gone
Come back when it's dawn.

I need your sweet Spirit
So that I can still bear it.
My life's turned around
I want to smile, but up comes a frown.

Lord, my help is only in You
No good thing to fret and stew.
When my heart is poured out
There's no time for doubt.

I will go to your Word
Where much comfort is heard.
Then sing a song….
And my heart will be strong.

*The righteous cry, and the Lord heareth, and delivereth them out of all their troubles.*
Psalm 34:17

# JOY COMES IN THE MORNING

Many times we wonder
If the night will ever end.
We've prayed and we've believed
Our heart to surely mend.

Lord, your Word reminds us
In the morning joy will be.
We must first endure the night
Then we will clearly see.

We will see that we have grown
Deep within our spirit.
We have put our trust in Jesus
His power helps us bear it.

*Weeping may endure for a night, but joy cometh in the morning.*
Psalm 30:5b

# GOD'S GREETING CARD

Many times things happen
You just don't understand
You feel like you're walking
On sinking sand.

You ask the Lord
For explanation
Praying He'll do
A transformation.

Words get twisted
Hearts are broken
Only God's love
Can be the token.

When you can't understand
And the way seems hard
Let His Word be
Your faithful greeting card.

*I wait for the Lord, my soul doth wait, And in His Word do I hope.*
Psalm 130:5

*Therefore I will look unto the Lord: I Will wait for the God of my salvation: my God will hear me.*
Micah 7:7

# PRAYER WHEN SICK

Lord, I'm sitting here
All alone.
My body is aching
I'm in the ill zone.

I try to pray
But even that's weak.
You hope that someone's
Called to speak.

Called by the Spirit
To speak out in prayer
Surely the Lord
Will send someone to care.

A few days later
Someone comes by.
They say, "I've been praying for you
But didn't know why."

If we trust in God's plan
Even in illness...
He'll speak to hearts
Out of the stillness.

*Wait on the Lord: be of good courage, and He shall strengthen thine heart: wait, I say on the Lord.*
Psalm 27:14

*I waited patiently for the Lord; and He inclined Unto me and heard my cry.*
Psalm 40:1

# A PRECIOUS PAGE

The chapter of mourning
Has come to an end.
A precious new page
Was turned to mend.

My heart has been mended
By the Lord above.
God sent me someone
That I could love.

A love so deep
It could only be
Planned by my Father
Just for me.

God cares so much.
More than we know.
He sees us through trials
Helps us grow.

He'll be there for you
If you ask Him to.
He's waiting to turn
A precious page for you.

*Thou hast turned my mourning into Dancing: thou hast put off my sackcloth, And girded me with gladness.*
Psalm 30:11

*He healeth the broken in heart, and Bindeth up their wounds. The Lord taketh pleasure in them that*
*Fear Him, in those that hope in His mercy.*
Psalm 147:3, 11

Judy Frobose Asmus weds Jim Hill on Feb. 29, 2008

# A NEW CHAPTER

Many times throughout our days
Things keep changing, make new ways.
On our own, we cannot cope.
With our friend, Jesus, there is hope.

Maybe your best friend just died
So alone, you cried and cried.
You have turned the very last page
A new chapter is now on stage.

It could be a job that you have lost
You sit down and count the cost.
A new chapter can be very fearful
We still have hope even though it's tearful.

The Holy Spirit gives comfort to all
Be sure that on His name you call.
If you're one who's in the middle of change
Let God's wisdom help you rearrange.

*Be careful for nothing; but in every thing by prayer and supplication with
thanksgiving let your requests be made known unto God. And the peace
of God, which passeth all understanding, shall keep your hearts and
minds through Christ Jesus.*
Philippians 4:6, 7

# THIS WEDDING DAY I PROMISE

This wedding day I promise to our Lord and then to you
That I will be forever faithful, true.
I'll respect you, encourage you and love you day by day.
For our Lord will always make a way.

Chorus:

In the good times and the bad, if we're happy or if we're sad
We will face each day together, on our knees.

In the good times and the bad, if we're happy or if we're sad
We will face each day together, hand in hand.

We will take all of our challenges and pray help from above
Our Jesus never leaves us. He always gives us love.
All our loneliness and sorrow have melted into peace
Since God ordained our meeting, our joy will never cease.

Repeat Chorus:

Judy wrote a song, "This Wedding Day I Promise,"
and sang it for Jim on their wedding day, 2/29/08

Jim & Judy had a vintage family wedding which included all of their 15 grandchildren and some of their children. Her wedding gown was an authentic 1930s wedding dress. Each of the girls wore a different vintage year dress, and the guys wore vintage vests.

# TEENAGER RULES OR TEENAGERS RULE

## by Tee Stuppiello

*Teenager Rules or Teenagers Rule* is a lighthearted, fun and real look at issues teens are dealing with today. It is filled with stories and "rules" acting as advice to help make it easier for pre-teens and teenagers to get through some of the most difficult times a girl may have to go through. Coming from the viewpoint of other teenagers, girls can easily relate to the stories and lessons that are meant to encourage self-esteem and make them aware of their own unique beauty, strength and the understanding they are not alone. With eight chapters in total, each created as a "handbook," they contain insightful, fun tales and "rules" to follow on being popular, being beautiful, getting away with lies, making a boy jealous, making a best friend, dealing with bullies and other teenage situations.

*Paperback, 61 pages*
*6" x 9"*
*ISBN 1-60672-805-9*

## About the author:

Tee Stuppiello spent her childhood in central New Jersey where she resides with her daughters, Melody and Toni Lee, and fiancé, Bryan. The idea for *Teenager Rules or Teenagers Rule* came to her while spending time with her teenage daughter and her friends on a snowy winter day. She is in the process of writing *Teenagers Volume 2* and other stories.

Also available from PublishAmerica

# SERENITY ISLE

## by Adriana Vasquez

*Serenity Isle* is for the angry soul, the bitter heart that wonders for the answers in life. Healing is the question, the deepest sentiment within our heart waiting to explode from within. Emotions throughout life with love, with parents, with life as a whole that leaves scars in our heart. These poems comment meaningfully on life's sorrows, depressions and its hard moments…

The purpose is to help the reader see things the way life is, and despite all the problems we have in life it reassures the reader there is a light at the end of the tunnel.

*Paperback, 132 pages*
*5.5" x 8.5"*
*ISBN 1-60610-509-4*

**About the author:**

Adriana Vasquez Becerril was born in New York City. She currently works as a school principal in the Bronx, with a Ph.D. in school leadership from St. Johns University. Adriana has written other books like *Passages of Life*.

Available to all bookstores nationwide.
www.publishamerica.com

# Bars, Beam, Floor, Vault, Death
## by Diana Danali

Bars, Beam, Floor, Vault, Death is the story of a mother's need to bring to justice the gymnastics coach who abused her young daughters. Morgan Jensen, Kate Anderson, and Julie Murphy tolerate Tom Connor's cruelty for some time before realizing that he is practicing mind control on their innocent daughters. After finally rescuing their daughters from him, while risking their lives, they embark on a mission to discover who he really is and stop his evil ways. While on their journey of discovery they learn that he has changed his name and is a suspect in the murder of an eleven-year-old girl who trained at his former gymnastics facility. The three women encounter people from his past and gain the information they need to put an end to his abuse. They return to Colorado thinking they have enough evidence to confront the coach. However, Tom Connor proves to be more cunning than they had ever imagined.

Paperback, 160 pages
5.5" x 8.5"
ISBN 1-60610-467-5

**About the author:**

Diana Danali was born and raised in Canon City, Colorado, and has lived there most of her life. She was a gymnastics instructor for two years. For the past twelve years she has been a Curves multi-club owner and for two of those years she was also a mentor for Curves International, Inc. She opened the thirteenth Curves club in the world in Canon City in 1996. With the help of Curves International, Inc., she was instrumental in installing Curves circuits in the five women's correctional facilities in Colorado. She is currently working on her second manuscript.